Computers in the English Classroom

A Primer for Teachers

Sally N. Standiford
University of Illinois at Urbana-Champaign

Kathleen Jaycox
Morton College, Chicago

Anne Auten
ERIC Clearinghouse on Reading and
Communication Skills

ERIC Clearinghouse on Reading and Communication Skills
National Institute of Education

National Council of Teachers of English
1111 Kenyon Road, Urbana, Illinois 61801

NCTE Editorial Board: Arthur N. Applebee, Thomas L. Clark, Julie M. Jensen, Elisabeth McPherson, Zora Rashkis, John C. Maxwell, *ex officio*, Paul O'Dea, *ex officio*

Book Design: Tom Kovacs for TDK Design

NCTE Stock Number 08180

Published 1983 by the ERIC Clearinghouse on Reading and Communication Skills, 1111 Kenyon Road, Urbana, Illinois 61801, and the National Council of Teachers of English, 1111 Kenyon Road, Urbana, Illinois 61801.

This document was prepared with funding from the National Institute of Education, U.S. Department of Education, under contract no. 400-78-0026. Contractors undertaking such projects under government sponsorship are encouraged to express freely their judgment in professional and technical matters. Prior to publication, the manuscript was submitted to the National Council of Teachers of English for critical review and determination of professional competence. This publication has met such standards. Points of view or opinions, however, do not necessarily represent the official view or opinions of either the National Council of Teachers of English or the National Institute of Education.

Library of Congress Catalog Card Number: 83-61710

Contents

Foreword

The Educational Resources Information Center (ERIC) is a national information system developed by the U.S. Office of Education and now sponsored by the National Institute of Education (NIE). It provides ready access to descriptions of exemplary programs, research and developmental efforts, and related information useful in developing more effective educational programs.

Through its network of specialized centers or clearinghouses, each of which is responsible for a particular educational area, ERIC acquires, evaluates, abstracts, and indexes current significant information and lists this information in its reference publications.

ERIC/RCS, the ERIC Clearinghouse on Reading and Communication Skills, disseminates educational information related to research, instruction, and personnel preparations at all levels and in all institutions. The scope of interest of the clearinghouse includes relevant research reports, literature reviews, curriculum guides and descriptions, conference papers, project or program reviews, and other print materials related to all aspects of reading, English, educational journalism, and speech communication.

The ERIC system has already made available—through the ERIC Document Reproduction Service—much informative data. However, if the findings of specific educational research are to be intelligible to teachers and applicable to teaching, considerable bodies of data must be reevaluated, focused, translated, and molded into an essentially different context. Rather than resting at the point of making research reports readily accessible, NIE has directed the separate clearinghouses to work with professional organizations in developing information analysis papers in specific areas within the scope of the clearinghouses.

ERIC/RCS is pleased to cooperate with the National Council of Teachers of English in making *Computers in the English Classroom: A Primer for Teachers* available.

Bernard O'Donnell
Director, ERIC/RCS

Introduction

Among Aesop's many fables is the one about the fox and the lion. In that tale, the fox—upon first meeting the lion—is so frightened that he nearly dies. He survives, though, for a second meeting. At the second meeting, he is still alarmed, but to a lesser extent. By the time of his third meeting with the lion, the fox is sufficiently confident to begin a conversation.

MORAL: Acquaintance softens prejudices.

At one time or another, it is easy for all of us to behave as the fox did in the fable. Teachers who have seen the rise and fall of programmed instruction, teaching machines, "back to basics" movements, and various other educational fads cannot help but fear what, at first meeting, seems to be another passing fancy in academia. If one has found a methodology that works, what is the sense of disrupting the *status quo*?

For many—if not most—teachers, computers represent an alien form of instruction. They are unknown, and they are threatening—just as was the lion to the fox. Nevertheless, teachers do have motivations to "soften prejudice." For one thing, because of the proliferation of high technology, computers are increasingly familiar to *students*. Professional pride is motivating many of us to scurry in order to stay one step ahead of our students. More important, computers represent an additional educational medium. Through them, it is possible to provide information or to manage instruction in ways otherwise unavailable to students.

Our premise is simply this: The decision "to use or not to use" computers in the English classroom should be an *informed* decision. It should be based upon an instructor's knowledge of what the computer can and cannot do, rather than upon fear or ignorance about computers.

What Can the Computer Do?

The computer can provide one-to-one instruction—if necessary, repeating information or offering examples for hours without losing patience or varying moods. It can incorporate student's responses into this instruction, branching to a reiteration if necessary—or advancing to a higher level of instruction if the learner seems competent to handle such progression. It can telescope time, allowing learners to experience events through simulations. It can use graphics to reinforce abstract concepts. Most important, it can store vast amounts of data and manipulate that data with incredible speed. This is what allows the flexibility of instruction. It is also what provides the potential for evaluative applications—analyzing student performance (How many people missed question one? How many times was option C chosen?) and recording each learner's accomplishments (How many people have completed unit one? How many succeeded during their first attempt?)

However, there are important things the computer cannot do. The computer can do nothing more than it is programmed to do. It cannot replace the human interactions that make each classroom unique. It cannot counsel a troubled student or banter about this morning's headline or last night's late movie. And, it cannot direct reflective discussion or test (as yet) the higher levels of learning (assimilation, evaluation, synthesis, analysis).

The value of the computer lies in the fact that it provides *one more tool* for the teacher to use. It frees the teacher from certain mundane chores so that instructional time is better utilized. Classroom teachers, ultimately, have the responsibility for all instructional decisions. (Do we "plow ahead," hoping the slower learners will catch up; or do we slow down? Do I lecture or does the class work in small groups? Do I use the text available, even though it's out of date, or do I generate my own materials?) Classroom teachers cannot begin to decide whether or not to use computer-assisted instruction until they become, at minimum, "computer literate."

What Do English Teachers Teach?

Traditionally, the study of English at the secondary level has had the three-fold foundation of language, literature, and composition. We encourage our students to understand the history of their language and the system of rules by which it operates (spelling, grammar, punctuation). We introduce them to the excitement reading can present—meeting characters both fictional and real, following those characters through simple or complex plot developments, and considering the impact of setting on the characters and the action. We help them to understand writing as a process, and we patiently advise them through prewriting, writing, and revising stages. In both their reading and their writing, we encourage students to explore values and emotions, as well as to appreciate the relationships among form, content, and style.

Depending upon grade level and curricular objectives, the content of "language" instruction may range from vocabulary development to spelling to grammar to linguistics to semantics. Fourth-graders might work on developing sentence structure: use of phrases, compound subjects or verbs, and so on. Junior high students might be developing a vocabulary with Greek and Latin root words, to accompany their study of mythology. At the high school level, a lesson on connotation and denotation may involve asking students to evaluate the distinctions between "athlete" and "jock," "hustler" and "hot dog." And in a college composition class, a lesson on style might incorporate all of those topics (sentence structure, vocabulary, connotation/denotation) to encourage maturity of writing style.

Similarly, the teaching of literature at various grade levels will incorporate the same basic elements over and over. In some courses, emphasis may be on genre: contrasting poetry with the short story, the novel, and the drama. In other courses, especially historical surveys, emphasis may involve relating the works and the lives of their authors to social and political developments of the period in which the works were written. In courses organized thematically, one particular issue, or theme, may be traced through a variety of works: poetry, short stories, novels—even film or television dramas. In any studies of literature, attention will always turn to essential elements: character, setting, plot, and theme (for prose); and rhythm, rhyme, meter, and theme (for poetry). At lower grade levels, questions may be directed toward simple comprehension (Who is the main character? Where does the story take place?). At higher grade levels, the teacher's questions will be directed toward more complex thinking skills (relating characterization to plot, or plot to the history of the era in which a work was written).

The teaching of composition also entails a "spiral" of curricular content. As students progress from elementary school to junior-high to high school and beyond, they will repeatedly encounter the concepts of unity, coherence, and emphasis—whether at the level of the single paragraph or with the multi-paragraph essay. Sentence structure, vocabulary, and punctuation will be topics of instruction repeatedly—as will the concepts of "main idea," "subordinate idea," "transitions," and "audience." The teaching of reading will involve many of these same concepts—but here the students are *perceiving* "main idea" or "subordination" or "style" in the writing of another, rather than producing it themselves.

This brief review of curriculum in the language arts contains no "revelations" for English teachers. It is simply a statement of "what we do." The *potential* revelation may come in considering the role computers *could* play in teaching these various aspects of the language arts curriculum. Consider the possibility of having one or more microcomputers within or adjacent to a classroom. Then consider the teacher who faces twenty-five or thirty students of varying levels of competence, each of whom is supposed to "master" certain speaking, reading, writing, and listening skills within the next sixteen weeks.

How can "that machine" help those students and their teacher achieve their goals? Most importantly, it can individualize. For the student who lags behind in ability to generate "standard usage" or who constantly confuses apostrophes with semicolons, it provides opportunities for endless tutoring or drill and practice—free time from the embarrassment of "being wrong" in the eyes of classmates or of stretching a teacher's patience to the limit when asking for a repeated explanation.

But the instructional applications of computers are not *limited* to drills or simple tutorial lessons. Programs asking open-ended questions can help students to generate ideas and to develop critical thinking skills in relation to literature. Text editors can help students to revise essays—adding, deleting, or rearranging—without the effort of rewriting "the WHOLE thing" (and running the risk of *making* an error in what was previously correct). Simulations and instructional games may serve as stimuli for writing—suggesting themes or characters or plot outlines—which would serve as "starting points" from which writers could generate essays, poems, or short stories. And beyond instruction, computers can provide instructional management: keeping records of "who has done what," testing, maintaining performance statistics, or even generating letters to students or parents offering records of students' academic activities.

Getting On with It

Computers *do* have applications within English classrooms. A teacher's decision whether or not to take advantage of those applications should be an *informed* judgment, reflecting the teacher's knowledge of both the operation of the hardware and the suitability of the software.

In the ensuing chapters, we will consider "computer basics" (defining "hardware" and "software" and the various capabilities of both); the various instructional *strategies* available via computers (it need not always be individualized instruction); examples of software reflecting these strategies, specifically in the language arts curriculum; and examples of various evaluation guidelines that instructors might use to judge the suitability of either hardware or software. To help us to move through these topics, each chapter will conclude with a scenario. The "cast of characters" reflects a composite of various English teachers we have all encountered at one time or another. They represent the entire spectrum of interest in computer-assisted instruction.

1 Computer Basics

You are probably the exception if you have not yet been affected by the use of computers in education. Although computers may not be used in your classroom (or even in your school), computers are affecting both *what* you teach and *how* you teach. In spite of this, many English teachers do not have a basic understanding of computers and their impact on society in general and education in particular. The purpose of this section is to explain, in as nontechnical a way as possible, what a computer is, how it works, and how it might be used to enhance instruction in the English classroom.

What's a Computer?

Computers come in a variety of shapes, sizes, and price tags. For some, the term *computer* may conjure up images of large, mysterious machines with banks of switches, dials, and pulsing lights and whirring, spinning disks. Others may think of only a large, fast calculating machine. In reality, a computer is a machine that can perform arithmetic operations but also has many, many more nonarithmetic functions, such as comparing, choosing, sorting, writing, and moving, which are needed to process, store, and retrieve large amounts of data. The advantage of the computer does not rest solely in the complexity or power of its operations but also in its quick, efficient, and reliable execution of those operations.

For our purpose, there are three "sizes" of computers that are of interest: maxi-, mini-, and micro-. In general, these sizes correspond directly to the amount of information and complexity of applications that the computer can process and the amount and kind of equipment that the computer can support. Large computers require (not surprisingly) a generous amount of physical space and special environmental conditions. They can store up to 16 million characters of information. Minicomputers often fit in large cabinets and operate in relatively "normal" environments. The usual limit of information that they can store is one million characters. Microcomputers, typically, can store between 4 thousand and 96 thousand characters of information.

1

Each of these types can have an important role in instruction. Your school district may use a large computer or a minicomputer for payroll, student scheduling, or attendance. Many school districts have classroom computer terminals connected to a large computer in the central office, as large computers can provide virtually immediate communication with many users at one time even though the users may be doing different things. Microcomputers also allow the user to interact directly with the computer. There is no need for time-sharing, however, because there is one computer for every user.

To better understand how a computer can process information rapidly and reliably, we should examine the primary components or units of virtually every computer system. These units are the processing unit, the input units, and the output units.

Processing Unit

The *processing unit* consists of the central processing unit (or CPU) and the main computer memory. The heart of the computer is the CPU. It contains all of the circuits needed to interpret instructions, perform operations, and control the input and output processes. In other words, the CPU is *the* computer in any computer system, whether it be a maxi-, mini-, or micro-. One important characteristic of the computer is the speed with which it can process information. Speed is critical in some data processing applications such as student scheduling, grade reporting, and payroll. The rate of processing is directly related to the size of the computer. In other applications, however, speed may not be as critical. For example, in many instructional lessons, much of the processing time depends upon the student (analyzing a poem, identifying a main idea in a paragraph) and, as a result, relatively longer computer processing times may not be significant.

A second characteristic of the processing unit, namely the amount of information that the computer can remember (or store), is important in almost every application. This *primary memory* can be used to hold three different kinds of information: the set of instructions that specifies the operations the computer is to perform (the program), the data that are being processed, and intermediate results that will be used later. The amount of information that can be stored is usually measured in *bytes* of information. A machine labeled 32K can store 32 thousand bytes or, approximately, 32 thousand characters of information. A double-spaced typed page holds approximately 2600 characters; so a 32K machine would hold roughly twelve-to-thirteen pages of text.

This primary memory is called *random access memory* or RAM. This memory is volatile in that the information stored in RAM can be changed, overwritten, or removed by appropriate instructions to the processing unit. In addition, all information stored there is lost when the machine is turned off.

There is another computer memory that is not volatile: the *read only memory* or ROM. The information in this memory is permanent and cannot be altered or destroyed. ROM is used to store programs and data that are needed in order for the computer and the person using the computer to communicate with each other. Since such programs must be protected if the computer is to be useful, this information is built into the computer when it is manufactured.

Input and Output Units

Input units and *output units,* collectively called I/O devices, are used to get information into and out of the computer. In most classroom applications, the usual input device is a keyboard that resembles a standard typewriter keyboard with additional special keys for communication with the computer. The usual output device is a cathode ray tube (CRT)—the type of tube used in a television set. A system that consists of a keyboard, CRT display, and a CPU is a complete computer system. It is, however, not a particularly convenient system for two reasons. First, the CRT display does not provide a permanent record of the output. (This can be remedied by using a printer as an output device.) Second, the system does not provide a way to store information between sessions.

When the machine is turned off, the information stored in RAM is lost. This means that programs and data must be reentered in subsequent sessions for which they are needed. In our minimal configuration (keyboard, CPU, and CRT) this means keyboard typing. However, most computer systems use secondary storage, which permits saving programs and data between sessions. Some common storage devices include cassette tapes and floppy disks that are made of a special material that can be magnetized. Information can be stored on the material as a pattern of electronic impulses, which can then be read directly into the computer's RAM.

To see how all of this might work, consider a typical application by a classroom teacher: averaging several grades for each student on the roster. Initially, a set of instructions to calculate grade averages would be entered into the computer through the keyboard. This program, now in primary memory, could then be read out to a floppy disk for permanent storage. The permanent copy of the program can then be used at any time without retyping it from the keyboard. Here is how it might work:

1. A *copy* of the grade averaging program is read into primary memory from the floppy disk. (The disk contains the program.)
2. The grades to be averaged are (probably) entered from the keyboard and are held in primary memory also.
3. The computer processes the grade data according to the instructions in the grade averaging program. Intermediate results, such as cumulative class averages are also stored in primary memory.
4. As each average is calculated it is displayed on the CRT screen.
5. A permanent record of the grade average is made by sending the output to a printer attached to the computer.
6. When the computer is turned off, the contents of primary memory are lost (the copy of the grade averaging program, the individual grades, and all intermediate results). In addition, the display on the CRT screen is gone. However, the disk still contains the program and the results can be recorded on printer paper.

This simple example illustrates all of the essential elements of input, processing, and output found in virtually every computer.

Computer Characteristics

Now that we have covered the basic elements of a computer, we will consider some of the "fine points" that distinguish one computer from another. These "fine points" are the characteristics that often become important to the classroom teacher because they involve the nature and readability of the information that can be input or output.

Text Display

Upper- and lowercase. Some computers allow the display and typing of both upper- and lowercase letters. Other microcomputers must have special adapters, which often replace the expected SHIFT key function with some other key. Even without the adapter, computers with graphics capabilities can use lessons that have upper- and lowercase letters. In these cases, however, student typed responses are usually in uppercase only. *Note:* The installation of some adapters may void the warranty or service contract.

Size of display. Typical CRT displays allow for approximately 1000 characters displayed on screens that range from 40–80 characters wide to 16–25 lines deep. (This paragraph has 710 characters: 65 characters wide and 11 lines deep.) In an instructional lesson, the screen display should be much less than the maximum allowed so that the displays are attractive and easy to read. On the other hand, word and text processing should allow for fuller display to give the typist some spatial clues about final format. Special accessories are available for increasing the usable screen width, but this generally reduces the resolution of individual characters. This may cause a problem for large group demonstrations.

Positioning text. Generally text is displayed starting at the top of the screen and continuing down to the bottom. Once the bottom is reached, additional text is added by moving all the other lines up one line. The top-most line is then "scrolled" off the display. In most computers it is possible to position text at a particular location rather than just at the next available line.

Special text effects. Many microcomputers display white letters on a black background. Some computers allow the reverse (black letters on a white background) or a flashing display that changes from the normal to the reverse. In most cases, different portions of the display can be in different display modes.

Overwriting one char/acter with another is usually not possible (such as the strike out of the letter "r" above). In this case, the original char/acter is replaced by the second, not combined with it. If you wanted to show a character that is the combination of two characters (such as '𝒓'), a special character would have to be designed.

Sized writing. A few computers will display bold letters. Usually all portions of the display are affected rather than just selected sections. Of course, use of sized writing decreases the amount of text that can be displayed.

Special characters. A few computers have "built-in" special characters (e.g., accent marks). Often, however, these characters must be specially designed using high resolution graphics (see below) directly or using specially designed programs. The use of subscripts, superscripts, and double strike characters often requires special design.

Graphics Display

Graphics resolution. Low resolution graphics is comparable to drawing a picture on a piece of graph paper. If a line of the drawing passes through any part of the grid, the entire grid is filled in. In low resolution a diagonal line would appear "saw toothed." High resolution graphics allows for drawing from one point to another point rather than from grid to grid. High resolution graphics are often used to design special characters. Several computers use graphics characters in place of either high or low resolution graphics. In these cases, the display is governed by the text displays, but the specific characters are selected to form a "picture."

HIGH RESOLUTION   LOW RESOLUTION

Color. Many computers will allow colored graphics. The number of usable colors varies with the computer. Only a few will permit colored text. Mixing text and graphics, however, sometimes causes normally white letters to have some color and lose some of their resolution.

Sound

Synthesizers. Several computers can generate sounds through speakers either in the computer or in the CRT monitor. Many computers will support special accessories to generate voice and/or music.

Audio. Instructional lessons can often be enhanced through the use of audio messages to accompany the visual display. Several computers will allow the concurrent use of audio and video. Usually the use of the audio must be coordinated by the user cued by messages of what to do (e.g., "Press the play button now"). A few will have the device under computer control.

Special Input Devices

Touch panels. Special panels can be installed around the CRT screen that, with appropriately designed lessons, permit the student to touch designated areas of the display rather than type responses at the keyboard. This may be helpful with younger children who are not facile with a typewriter keyboard.

Joysticks/game paddles. These accessories are often used to position graphics characters on the CRT screen. Although their use is associated with arcade games, when used in conjunction with carefully designed lessons they can make computers more accessible to orthopedically disabled students.

Graphics tablets. Drawings and pictures can be "traced" and displayed on the screen. The images can then be saved and incorporated into instructional lessons, thus bypassing high-resolution graphics programming.

Optical scan (mark sense). Mark sense cards can be used to input test results, grades, or attendance, for example, rather than typing the data.

Special Output Devices

Printer. Many computer applications require or are enhanced by using a printer for a record of the output (called "hard copy"). Some of the factors that should be considered when selecting a printer include quality of the output, locations of the printer when in use, and the amount of use the printer will have.

Letter-quality printers use either typeballs or "daisy wheels" that produce output similar to that of a high quality typewriter. The typeballs or daisy wheels are imprinted with individual characters that are positioned correctly by the printer as they strike the paper one character at a time. The typeballs or daisy wheels can be changed to give different type styles. This paragraph was printed with a letter quality printer.

DOT MATRIX PRINTERS DO NOT USE PRE-FORMED CHARACTERS. INSTEAD, THE CHARACTERS TO BE PRINTED ARE FORMED BY SELECTING PORTIONS OF A MATRIX OF WIRES. THE SELECTED WIRES EXTEND FROM THE MATRIX TO PRINT ON THE PAPER. FOR EXAMPLE, TO PRINT THE CHARACTER '3' USING A 5 X 7 GRID, THE PATTERN MIGHT LOOK LIKE THIS:

SOME ADVERTISING SIGNS OR TIME AND TEMPERATURE DISPLAYS USE A MATRIX OF LIGHTS TO FORM CHARACTERS. THE DOT MATRIX PRINTER USES THE SAME PRINCIPLE. THIS PARAGRAPH WAS TYPED WITH A DOT MATRIX PRINTER.

One advantage of dot matrix printers is that printing is not restricted to preformed characters. Any pattern of dots from the matrix may be printed, as there are more than 34 billion possibilities. A possible disadvantage is that the quality of print is not as good as typewriter print since the individual dots are distinguishable. Also, some of the lowercase letters that normally drop below the line (such as p, g, y) are written entirely above the line.

Both letter quality printers and many dot matrix printers are impact printers in that a mechanical device must strike the paper to make the impression. Such printers can make multiple copies but they are very loud. As a result, the noise may make inclass use difficult if not impossible. An alternative might be to have a nonimpact printer that uses heat to "burn" an image on special paper or to use a plotter type printer that draws the characters in special ink that dries immediately on contact with the paper.

Video projection units. Classroom demonstrations are often hampered by difficulty in viewing the small display screen. Special projection units have been developed to project the CRT display to a screen much like the image from an overhead projector.

Communications

Modem. The modulator-demodulator is a device that is used for telephone communications between a computer and a terminal.

Networking. Networking allows one computer to send output to or receive input from other terminals or computers in the network. In this way, a teacher's terminal could be used to send different lessons to different students and in turn receive status reports from each student. In addition, there needs to be only a single copy of each lesson, which can be loaded at the teacher's station and sent to as many students as necessary.

Languages

A number of languages are used for programming instructional lessons. Each language has characteristics that make it more (or less) suited for a particular application. Regardless of the language, some striking parallels exist between programming languages and the English language (Dennis and Auten, 1982).

Vocabulary
English: a well-developed vocabulary promotes clear, precise communication.

Programming: good languages permit the definition of new vocabulary.

Grammar
English: system of word-forms and word-order allow word classification by use.

Programming: words (commands) are classified according to their use in one of three classifications: action, branching, and looping.

Syntax
English: the way that words are put together and related to each other in sentences, sentence structure.

Programming: same as above with the forms rigidly defined.

Punctuation
English: clarifies meaning of sentences.

Programming: used to set-off words to aid automated parsing.

Structure
English: the standard five paragraph theme or the Haiku poem.

Programming: the main procedure contains the basic task; subprocedures have similar structure to paragraphs and function accordingly.

Readability
English: clarity and cohesiveness derived from previous points.

Programming: needed to recover through processes involved; also depends on previous points.

Classroom Environments

Computers can be used in a variety of ways in a classroom ranging from large group to individual use. An excellent and reasonably flexible computer system for classroom instruction would consist of the following elements:

> 48K RAM
>
> full-sized keyboard
>
> single disk drive (two would be better)
>
> printer
>
> video monitor or television

Using the computer for word or text processing might require additional hardware accessories, such as:

> upper-lower case adapter
>
> video text display to increase display
>   width to approximately eighty characters

Classroom Setting

Classroom use. It is often necessary to connect several monitors (CRTs) together so that all students can view the display. Some computers do not permit the use of more than one monitor. If the monitor or the computer has an external *video jack,* additional monitors can be used.

Be sure that the material used in large group discussions has sufficient resolution to be viewed comfortably. Often it is necessary to turn out the lights, making note-taking difficult. Setting up for a large group is not difficult, but it does require advanced planning to be sure that all the equipment is available and can be used properly.

Individual workstation. The concern is that the monitor is placed so that the student can view it comfortably for the required time. Some display screens will reflect classroom lights; others have some distortions at the corners. There should be sufficient work area and storage so that tapes and disks are not placed on top of equipment (which may threaten their reliability) when not in use.

Environment. Computer equipment should be kept in a dust-free (particularly chalk dust-free) area that is not subject to extreme temperature and humidity variations. It is best to keep the equipment covered when not in use, away from chalk dust, smoke, and excessive changes in temperature and humidity.

Chapter 1 Scenario

As an illustration of the manner in which these computer character-istics can become important to the classroom teacher, consider the case of Duane Ridley.*

In response to a request from Professor Richards at the college, Mr. Ridley agreed to allow a demonstration of computer-assisted instruction in his eighth-period Freshman English class. Announce-ment of this special event brought raves from his students, who immediately envisioned fifty minutes of "Pac-Man" or "Dungeons and Dragons"—games immensely popular at the computer arcade in the shopping mall. A few curious faculty members also asked if they could attend the demonstration. (Their requests were greeted with gusto from Mr. Ridley, who immediately realized the disciplinary value of two or three extra "teacher presences" in the room.)

The day was not atypical for Duane Ridley—Murphy's Law was being reaffirmed every time he turned around. The endless ques-tions, beginning with the first period of the day, had been anticipated ("Hey, Mr. Ridley, is it true that you're taking your eighth hour class to the shopping center arcade?" "Mr. Ridley, surely you don't expect to bring a computer into an English class! Mr. Cook and I have managed to teach English for more than seventy years (between us) without resorting to folderol and gimcrackery . . .").

What had not been anticipated was Professor Richards' early arrival and his concomitant request to set up demonstration materials, effectively destroying the lesson plan of the seventh-period English Literature class, which was in the midst of a heated debate about the universality of "The Beastie" in Lord of the Flies.

As soon as all hope had been given up for salvation of that seventh-period class and Professor Richards had begun setting up his hardware, the logic of the "anti-computer people" started to clarify itself to Duane. First, there were problems regarding access to elec-trical outlets—until the most fleet-footed student in class departed in search of the Chief of Maintenance, Guardian of All Extension Cords. Second, Professor Richards had been limited (by time, space, and physical strength) to bringing in only one microcomputer and two

---

*Duane Ridley teaches high school English (freshmen and seniors) at the public high school of a moderately sized midwest college town. He also teaches Composi-tion I (part-time) at the college. He has an M.A. in English, has been teaching for ten years (only two of them in this town), and serves as freshman class moderator. He has been approached by the college to employ computer-assisted instruction in his high school classes on an experimental basis; he is curious to know more before deciding.

CRT screens. This resulted not only in the need to move a lot of furniture (so that all students could see a screen), but also in a chorus of typical students' complaints ("I thought we were each going to have a computer to work on!" or "I can't see through Freddy's big head!"). Professor Richards allowed himself only a few seconds to wish that he had brought along the college's newly acquired video projection unit.

Despite these problems, Duane and Professor Richards were able to get the hardware set up and the programs loaded. After the professor had gained the students' attention by allowing a half dozen of them to operate various programs, complete with color graphics, he then asked for a volunteer who would utilize a new program just written by one of the graduate students at the college. The program was more complex than the simple grammar drills and tutorials that Duane and his colleagues had seen in previous displays. Through a series of branching operations, it allowed students to review instructional concepts or to be tested with alternate sets of questions. The instructional quality of the program proved very impressive not only to Duane and the other teachers present, but even to the student volunteer who was using the program.

What proved frustrating to everyone concerned, however, was the program's inability to distinguish uppercase from lowercase letters. To a room holding three English teachers, a program that did not penalize the student for omitted capitalization was clearly not adequate. This, combined with the program's requirement for certain routines to be rigidly followed in the student's response pattern, led to a few suggestions for revision of the program.

Despite these flaws in the software and the headaches associated with the arrangement of hardware, the professor's visit was rated an overall success by everyone involved. He felt happy that he could offer some concrete suggestions for revision to the graduate student programmer. The students were enthusiastic about the idea that classtime could be spent utilizing computers. And Duane Ridley, along with his colleagues, felt a new enthusiasm for the potential of computer-assisted instruction. He had seen participation in this class from students who had previously been nonparticipants, including bright-but-bored Alex Morrow and the incredibly shy Donna Jackson. His colleagues were heard to comment about the value of patience— as the program repeated the explanation of a single concept in four different contexts until the student user finally grasped its message and responded appropriately. They were also impressed with the idea that computer-assisted instruction could be available in early morning or late afternoon hours, when the teachers themselves were usually wrapped up in committee meetings or supervision of extra-curricular activities. Most important, they had been quite taken by Professor Richards' explanation of the record-keeping and record-management facilities available in other programs. The possibility of turning over to computers the chores of record-keeping and grade-averaging made their faces glow in anticipation.

As Professor Richards and a few student volunteers carted the equipment back to the college van, everyone agreed it had been a worthwhile afternoon.

2 Instructional Strategies

Computers are used in the classroom in three different ways: as the focus of instruction (i.e., teaching *about* computers), as the delivery medium of instruction (i.e., teaching *with* computers), and as the manager of instruction. Although it may seem that the English teacher is not concerned with "teaching about," some of the classroom applications will require a basic familiarity with that function. Chapter 1 discussed some of these points. In discussing "teaching with" a computer, we should keep in mind that computers can be used to deliver the primary instruction or can be used to support instruction by providing either remediation or enrichment. Whether the computer provides delivery or support, the teacher retains the role of instructional decision-maker and, as such, must design ways to integrate the computer into the conventional curriculum.

To aid in this integration, this chapter will focus on instruction in general and then apply those principles to computerized instruction. In addition, we will discuss some of the attributes that should be reflected in good computer applications to the teaching of language arts.

The computer delivers instruction in accord with the four components of a complete teaching episode: presentation of material, questioning, student response, and reinforcement or corrective feedback. A complete teaching episode can be very short:

> Teacher (pointing): This is the letter *a*. (presentation)
> Teacher (pointing): What is this? (question)
> Student: The letter *a*. (response)
> Teacher: Very good. (feedback)

Or it can be very long (as when the college professor lectures for the entire semester, gives a final exam, and posts the grades). The length of the teaching episode will often depend upon the maturity of the students. As students become (or are expected to be) responsible for their own learning, the teaching episodes become longer. Regardless of the length of the teaching episode, however, a complete episode will contain the four components.

Computerized Instruction

These four components are essential to computerized instructional lessons. In addition, the use of the computer adds two other components normally under the control of the teacher: review of material and the path taken by the student. Altogether the six components of computerized instruction include presentation, questioning, judging, feedback, review, and routing. Let us consider these as they relate to computers.

Presentation. The presentation of material is usually done through the use of definitions, examples, rules, and nonexamples. When computerized, the fundamental sequence should be designed for the student who is able to grasp and demonstrate knowledge of the indicated skills. Instruction should be kept to a minimum. Additional information, explanation, and applications should be included but presented only for students who need or request it.

The computer as a delivery medium suggests that information should be presented in limited amounts, with attractive and quickly plotted screen displays. Although novelty displays are positively correlated with attention, frequent repetition loses the "novelty" effect quickly.

Questions. Each skill/knowledge implied by the objectives should be tested at the appropriate level. Questions should be germane only to the material in the current or related teaching episode. Rhetorical questions are inappropriate (don't you agree?). The common forms of questions which can be effectively computerized include true-false, multiple choice, fill-in, and short answer questions, as well as those appearing on touch sensitive panels that call for nonverbal response.

Questions are most often used to determine whether or not a student "knows" the material we have taught and to give that student a grade. We make most of our instructional decisions based on our assessments of student comprehension. For example, at the extreme, we may give enrichment materials to "excellent" students so they won't be bored while we work with the others; or we give extra help to "poor" students and hope that they can catch up. Almost always, these decisions are based on our assessments of what the students know or don't know relative to our questions. Although assessment of student comprehension is important and necessary, there is another dimension which we should also consider: a student's awareness of his or her own comprehension.

Regardless of whether or not a student is "doing well" (by whatever grading scheme we use), a student may or may not be aware of his or her own understanding. Students have accurate comprehension awareness when they realize they know or do not know. On the other hand, students have inaccurate comprehension awareness if they are not sure or are unaware that they do or do not know. Inaccurate comprehension awareness may be exhibited in several ways: students who have unjustified feelings that they have the material "down pat," students who are sure they just "blew" the test (on which they get top scores), or students who just haven't thought about their own state of knowledge. When we put these comprehension/comprehension awareness dimensions together we divide our students into four groups.

Comprehension

high	low	
know and are aware they know	do not know and realize they do not know	high
1	2	
3	4	Comprehension Awareness
know but think they don't	do not know but think they do	low

Our main goal as teachers is to have all of our students in Cell 1. Although we may occasionally have students who seem to be born to this cell, it is more likely we will be called on to devise strategies to move students from the other cells to Cell 1. The selection of an effective, efficient strategy will depend upon which cell the student is in initially. In all cases, however, the strategy should be based on the use of appropriate questioning techniques.

For students in Cell 2, questions and feedback designed to help the student apply appropriate studying strategies and techniques are effective (for example, SQ3R). These students do not gain from feedback that simply indicates they are wrong—they already know that. Cell 3 students need positive reinforcement. Although research has demonstrated the overall ineffectiveness of telling students they are correct, to do so is effective for this subset of students since their lack of confidence is a critical attribute. This group of students is often overlooked in our teaching strategies because we tend to focus on the comprehension dimension—and these students are doing satisfactorily on that dimension.

The approach for students in Cell 4 should be directed first at breaking the false feeling of "knowing" rather than at teaching content. You cannot teach a student if the student thinks he or she already knows. One approach might be to ask questions directed at having the student recognize a contradiction between what the student really knows and what the student thinks he or she knows (but doesn't). For example, the student may use the pronoun "I" incorrectly as in the use of the object of a preposition in the sentence "The letter was addressed to Jim and I." The student remembers learning to name others first when referring to a group in which he or she is included, and so uses "Jim and I" instead of "me 'n' Jim." Having been told that "Jim and I" is correct usage, he or she believes it to be correct in all cases and is difficult to convince that in this instance, "Jim and me" is the correct form. Through carefully designed questions, this false confidence can be shaken and instruction resumed.

By using appropriate questions and feedback, the computer can often enhance instruction designed for these different groups of students. It must be noted, however, that it is often "expensive" in both time and money to develop complex programs to address these different needs. The design and programming effort required begins to take advantage of the medium in a creative and effective way.

Response. Students must be made aware that they are to respond and must be told how to respond. Frequently, the students are learning both new content and new skills related to computer use. Occasionally, they are unable to answer a question because of the environment—not the content. For example, the student might be required to type an accent mark which is not marked on the keyboard. The student must be given instructions on how to type that mark, and the instructions should be retrievable at the time they may be needed.

Judging. There are four classes of answers that students might give to any question: the correct (or synonymous) answer; answers which are literally incorrect but conceptually correct (misspellings *might* be included here); the classes of anticipated wrongs that reflect the mislearning of students (for example, identifying a dependent clause as a complete sentence); and the unanticipated but not necessarily wrong answers. Each of these contingencies must be planned for in advance in computerized instruction. In the conventional learning environment, the teacher can make immediate judgments of answers not planned for. The computer is unable to ad-lib judgments. The computer program must be sensitive to a wide variety of student responses if it is to be individualized. The feedback for the student will be based on these categories of answers.

Feedback. Feedback for correct answers should be directed at reinforcement of the concepts and should be included for those students with low confidence. Feedback for incorrect responses might take on several forms:

1. ignore the mistake
2. tell the student he or she is wrong
3. tell the student he or she is wrong and give the correct answer
4. tell the student he or she is wrong and explain why the answer is wrong
5. tell the student he or she is wrong, give the correct answer, and explain why the answer is correct

Each of these has a role in computerized instruction. It is important to note, however, that options 1 and 2 are least productive if they are the only options used in a testing situation. Option 3 has been shown to be effective in many research studies. One must be sure that the student is not expected or allowed to copy a correct answer as the only requirement for proceeding, as that would allow the student to become passive. Students should be made to respond actively before being told the correct answer. Lessons should be designed so that the incentive is for students to answer correctly. Options 4 and 5 represent more elaborate correction procedures with 4 requiring sophisticated diagnosis of the student error. Students' knowledge should be sufficiently tested to insure that objectives have been attained. New but equivalent questions should be asked or the missed questions should be repeated.

Finally, the feedback for unanticipated responses should include some directions on how to formulate an expected answer. The response should always be acknowledged as unexpected—not as incorrect.

Review. Many instructional lessons allow the student to review previously presented material. This is particularly important if the student is unable to complete the lesson in one session. Ideally, long lessons should not require the student to begin again. One strategy might be to ask the student some questions related to already studied material followed by an option or a recommendation to review before starting the new material.

Routing. Lessons will vary on the degree of student control over the sequence of material. Ideally, all lessons should allow options to review, request additional explanations or examples, answer additional questions, and progress at the student's rate. Control over the sequence of topics may or may not be up to the student.

Occasionally, students who lack the prerequisite skills may enter the computer lesson. Ideally, lessons should test for entry behaviors and provide appropriate feedback for students who lack the required skills. It is up to the teacher using the lesson to identify the skills needed and to use the lesson appropriately with his or her students.

It should now be clear that a computer can reinforce student learning as a patient teacher, allowing repeated mistakes, providing alternative explanations or examples.

Teaching Strategies

Given this understanding of the various components of instruction, we can now focus on the teaching strategies that utilize those components.

There are a variety of teaching strategies that we can use to enhance all or some of these components as explained in the following pages. For example, a "tutorial" approach will embody all of the instructional components, often offering several complete teaching episodes. A "drill-and-practice" strategy, on the other hand, will generally stress the evaluation aspect of question, response, and feedback and omit presentation, review, and routing as part of the drill-and-practice session. Definitions of the various instructional styles can be found in the glossary.

Regardless of the specific components of a particular teaching strategy, the classroom teacher is responsible for fitting the strategy into the "big picture" and should not consider it just in isolation. For example, it is not possible to effectively use or evaluate a drill-and-practice session without considering the entire teaching episode/context of which it is a part. This is particularly important when using computerized lessons which have been developed by other people. The teacher must detach it from the environment in which it was developed and consider it in the instructional context of the classroom.

While it's understood that the various instructional strategies do not exist in isolation in computer-assisted instruction, we do analyze them individually for purposes of communication. As we discuss the separate classifications, keep in mind that the primary criterion for evaluating a specific strategy should not be based on the label it is assigned, but rather on how it fits into the overall delivery of instruction.

At present, CAI is being used in the English classroom in three major ways: teaching with computers (using drill or practice lessons, tutorials, or dialogue systems involving problem solving or simulations), managing instruction (record keeping tasks), or using utility programs (word processing/text analysis/text editing). Some programs do not fit neatly into a single. category, but these categories are the easiest way to classify what is more accurately described as a continuum of complexity and varying programming techniques.

Teaching with Computers

Drill or practice. The vast majority of English lessons currently in use implement a drill or practice strategy. Given the fact that some English skills require repetition and some students require infinite patience, these programs do have real value, especially when the alternative is a programmed textbook or a school staff whose time is so limited that the student will receive insufficient help. An ideal drill or practice lesson is easily integrated with teacher-presented material and provides ample opportunity for a teacher to add to the drill items, such as vocabulary words specific to an assigned story. The lesson management section of the program then allows the teacher to add, substitute, or delete words, definitions, or context sentences for later student use or practice. Such a lesson offers responses that are appropriate to students' errors, a sequenced pattern of reinforcement for correct responses, an increased or decreased level of difficulty depending on students' responses, a review for incorrect responses, and the capability to retire those items the student has answered correctly a number of times. A good drill lesson is designed to handle misspellings with flexibility and to summarize students' performance at the end of the lesson.

Tutorials. The essential difference between drill or practice lessons and tutorials is that the former often work in a linear fashion and are chiefly designed to review already presented information. The latter, on the other hand, are designed to present information, ask questions over that information, and then present individually tailored responses to student answers through a technique called "branching." In effect, then, a computerized tutorial tries to simulate the dialogue between a tutor and a student. Tutorials are more difficult to write, since the programmer must anticipate all student responses, including all possible errors. In this way, the alternative presentations provided by the computer will always be appropriate to the individual student's level and ability. A good tutorial presents questions that follow logical progressions toward stated objectives and display questions after each screen of exposition. In a good writing heuristic, it is important that the questions be open ended. Student answers are judged with flexibility and, in response to wrong answers, additional information or clues are provided. The lesson provides frequent access to help or review and suggests any necessary remediation.

It is frequently the case that "good" (i.e., flexible, individualized, germane) tutorials do not exist for all content areas for which there are "good" drill and practice lessons. In these cases, the teacher must provide the learning environment. It is necessary, nevertheless, that there be an appropriate match between the tutorial and the drill or practice lesson. A tutorial lesson is used to define a context for learning specific material and to teach a student which responses are appropriate in that context. A drill lesson derived from the tutorial then provides a student the opportunity to practice making the appropriate correct responses.

Problem solving. Next along the spectrum of complexity and usefulness, more sophisticated tutorial programs have reached the level of dialogue systems, problem-solving programs capable of guiding a student through prewriting and writing processes. In the best of these programs, the computer seems to understand the student's responses and then prods him or her onto the next step in the composition process. The questions are realistic and sequenced toward specific goals. Feedback to students' decision making is immediate, and suggestions are offered for optimal performance. The lesson is designed to ask the student a question, to pick up a key word in the student's response (matching it to a preprogrammed list of words), and then, based on that key word, to ask another question that leads the student to further refine his or her answer. Such lessons require a computerized expert—a model of how a human expert would solve the problem. The student's current state is compared to and contrasted with the "expert" to determine the next best step. At this time, our ability to computerize the English language expert is very limited and, as a result, our problem-solving programs are primitive and restricted to small areas. In the area of composition, programs have been designed to replicate a thought-provoking dialogue between a master teacher and a student, but are less than ideal because of the limitations of both the program designer and of the computer on which the program runs.

For example, consider a prewriting dialogue program designed to help students prepare to write by asking a series of questions over student-selected topics. While performed satisfactorily enough in a limited way on a large mainframe or maxicomputer, the program plods along at an unacceptable and inappropriate rate when processed by one of today's microcomputers.

Other dialogue systems, designed to be used during the editing stage of writing, "read" essays that students type into the computer. The programs then respond to the student work in such limited areas as sentence length; excessive use of prepositions; and use of passive voice, forms of the verb *to be* or relative pronouns. A computer program can also serve as a spelling proofreader, but spelling words must be programmed either by the classroom teacher or in commercially prepared spelling dictionaries or software.

Utilities

Word processing/text editing. The pedagogical applications of text editing programs are particularly important in a world where students will do much of their professional writing on word processors and microcomputers. Those who opt to use a computer as a writing tool cite a number of benefits from doing so, in both composing and revising strategies. Initial writing blocks are overcome when working with a screen terminal and its ease of erasing through simple backspacing, a capability that often stimulates a flow of words that paper inhibits. Mechanical difficulties with poor handwriting and spelling are overcome when composing on a computer; the copy looks professional, boosting a writer's self-confidence; spelling is easily corrected after a first draft, causing writers to be more relaxed about putting words down. Because of the ease of revising without tedious recopying, writers are more open to suggestions for change and less inhibited about implementing suggestions. An ideal program in this area would provide clear instructions, easily implemented editing procedures, adequate text storage, access to help or to a review of directions, and a straightforward use of the keyset.

Another useful utility program in the production of writing is computerized text analysis. Programs designed as automated style guides can determine when a grammar rule is violated or when a writing style is turgid because of excessive use of passive voice verbs or prepositional phrases. Spelling checkers, spelling correctors, and readability indexes have all been automated to give a breakdown of some of the the things that might be wrong with an author's text.

Management aids. An additional mode for computer use in instruction is the one designed for program management and record keeping, often called computer managed instruction or CMI and used in all content areas. CMI systems are often used as pretests, study guides, or posttests. In all of these situations, a CMI system can provide diagnoses of students' difficulties, prescribe remediation, and schedule use of instructional resources. Ideal CMI programs offer clear directions, easy record modification, provision for adjusting learning parameters for individual students and whole classes, storage for individual student records, and privacy for those records.

The possibilities for offering a variety of teaching methods with a computer are limited only by the program designer's skill and creativity, coupled with the capability of the machine for which the software is written. The design of sophisticated, well-conceived and implemented lessons in any of the instructional modes discussed here is both challenging and possible.

Chapter 2 Scenario

The scenario to conclude this chapter brings together Karen Young,* our "pro-computer" activist, and Robert Inglewood,** whose sentiments are at the opposite end of the spectrum. In the course of

---

*Karen Young teaches junior high English in a metropolitan midwest school with an enrollment of approximately 1,300. She is completing requirements for her M.Ed. and has been teaching for five years. She is fascinated with the concept of computer-assisted instruction in English (the topic of her master's thesis) as a result of her good experiences with it in graduate classes.

**Robert Inglewood teaches high school junior and senior honors English at a relatively small suburban high school (enrollment approximately 2,000). He has an M.A. plus forty hours of graduate credit and has been teaching for thirty years, twenty-seven of them at this school. He has "put in his time" as chairman of the English department, doesn't enjoy teaching composition, and is violently opposed to the concept of using computers in the English classroom ("it isn't capable of teaching"; "it's a new-fangled bother"; it might teach some things better than he).

conducting the research for her master's thesis, Karen has decided to visit various secondary schools—some urban, some rural—to describe the extent to which computer-assisted instruction is being utilized in the different academic divisions. Mr. Inglewood has learned of her visit to his suburban institution and has made an appointment to confer with her in the faculty lounge during his free period.

After some preliminary small talk over coffee, Mr. Inglewood directs the discussion to Karen's research and her reason for being at McCormick High. Ever the gentleman, he refrains from outright disparaging remarks about computers or Karen's interest in them. Instead, he begins to recite for her the various "fads" he has seen come and go during his thirty years as an English teacher. He recalls the "practical" emphasis of the late 50s, the "relevance" of the 60s, and the mastery learning/programmed learning approaches of the 70s. He acknowledges that computers are certainly impressive; every time he goes to the bank or to the grocery store, he is grateful for the efficiency they provide to him as a consumer.

"But using them in an English class is another situation entirely," he notes. "In my class, the most frequent method of instruction is my lecture. Or, at times, the students work individually or in small groups. In any event, class sessions are a constant source of surprise. No matter how carefully I plan, I find I always need to make on-the-spot judgments about whether or not an objective is being met. If not, I need to adapt accordingly. The lesson plan that runs smoothly in a first-hour class may need total revamping with the third-hour class. Now, how could a computer—which is programmed to follow a particular instructional path—ever exhibit the flexibility needed in my classes? And furthermore, how can one microcomputer—or even two—provide instruction to a class of twenty to twenty-five students? The value of these gimmicks is supposed to lie in their ability to individualize instruction. But a 1:20 or even a 1:10 ratio is not individualizing. And I surely can't believe that our district is planning to buy these things in volume."

Karen listened thoughtfully to his remarks. She had to admit that his comments about individualization made sense, and she appreciated the perspective of history from which he viewed current events. "So he's not just an anti-everything old grouch," she thought to herself. Then, feeling the need to respond—especially in light of the fact that several other teachers in the lounge had been listening to Mr. Inglewood's remarks—she cleared her throat and began.

"You've made several good points, Mr. Inglewood. If I weren't so convinced that computers have a lot to offer, I might be persuaded by your remarks to get out my "Nuke Computers" signs and start protesting. Let me tell you how I feel.

"You're right about the fact that a teacher needs to make the judgments about when to speed up, when to slow down, and when to change direction entirely. You're also right about the idea that one computer and twenty students do not represent the ideal "individualization" setting.

"The major argument that I would offer is simply that the computer provides one additional instructional method—one more resource from which teachers can draw. As Lucy once said to Charlie Brown, referring to her fist, her five fingers collectively provided much more force than any of them would individually. This same principle is true when it comes to using computers in the classroom.

"Maybe only a handful of students, at any one time, will be working with it. Maybe the greatest value it will serve will involve only grammar drills or tutorials or the use of a word processor as students write essays. But if—in providing those services—the computer helps even a few students to master concepts which they might otherwise have failed to master, I feel we should be taking advantage of that opportunity."

Mr. Inglewood chuckled to himself as Karen finished. "The impassioned philosophy of youth," he thought. Aloud he said only, "Miss Young, I admire the strength of your feelings. I fear the enthusiasm which you display has long ago been lost on me. We still remain in opposing camps, but I believe we can be cordial antagonists. Most important, I think we both feel we're working for the good of our students."

3 Computer Applications to English

The initial rush to publish software to meet the demands of a rapidly expanding educational computing market produced computer programs for English and language arts instruction that could be generously described as less than ideal. Advancing computer technology will not resolve all of the limitations exemplified by those lessons. Many limitations are simply the result of our inexact characterization of the structure of the language.

What kind of computer applications are possible in language arts instruction then, and where are they available? And if they are possible, but not available, what then?

What's Possible

Most computer based instructional materials are traditional "frame-based" presentations. In this type of presentation, the lesson is laid out as a decision tree where the path taken by the student depends upon his or her response to questions at the branch points. The tree can be simple (linear) in that all students begin at the same point and ultimately end at the same point. Deviations from the linear flow are simply to correct incorrect responses made by the student:

Or the tree can be quite complex in that ending points will be different for students responding differently to questions along the way:

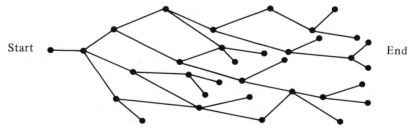

27

Most drill and practice lessons are examples of simple trees because the context in which the student is to respond has been defined by previous teaching. That is, the drill and practice lesson is not designed to teach new responses but simply to give students the opportunity to respond in well-defined ways. Within the four areas of English instruction that we will address—literature, composition, reading, and language arts—drill and practice lessons exist for almost every topic germane to the content areas. Most are limited, however, to lower levels of learning.

Decision trees for tutorials can range from simple to complex. The type depends upon the goals of instruction and the nature of the student-computer interaction. To illustrate, consider the area of composition. Lessons exist that explain the "how to," but there are few, if any, that adequately address the "when to." For example, sentence combining lessons teach how to combine two short sentences to make one longer sentence. In these lessons, the sentences are selected to clearly illustrate the procedures. Less well-defined issues such as style or emphasis are not addressed directly. In other words, the "when to" questions are generally avoided except for extreme cases when one "should always" or "should never."

Like tutorials, simulations and problem solving lessons can have decision trees ranging from simple to complex. Generally, these tend to the latter rather than to the former. Regardless of which tree-structure is used, the frame-based presentation of material requires the student to respond in ways anticipated by the lesson.

Information utility lessons, such as spelling or syntax checkers, judge student responses either by comparing the response to entries in a preprogrammed "dictionary" or by applying well-formulated rules. The misspelling of the word "quirk" as "qirk" could be identified form [sic] either a dictionary or by a rule about "u after q . . ." In the last sentence, the word "from" was misspelled as "form." In that case, a dictionary would not be sufficient to identify it since both are valid words. A parts-of-speech rule, however, might be able to spot it.

Most utilities present feedback as questions for the student to consider: Is [word] misspelled? Is the sentence with [phrase] passive? This form of feedback is used because either the dictionary comparison or the rule formulation might overlook or misclassify some responses. This limitation bears directly on our own understanding of the structure of the subject matter.

Some utilities can correct errors where there are well-formed rules. For example, it is possible for a utility to correct certain punctuation mistakes such as misuse of quotation marks.

Advantages of Frame-Based Instruction

The computer can continuously provide consistently presented instruction. For appropriate objectives and level of learning, it can provide an environment conducive to improved learning. The technical capabilities of the computer can simulate instruction not feasible in other environments.

Limitations of Frame-Based Presentations

Both the content domain and the current state of the technology limit computer applications in English. On one hand, many areas of the content domain cannot be specified by well-formulated rules or procedures that can be modeled on a computer. On the other hand, in areas where there are such rules, the relatively inefficient processing of the microcomputer often makes the student/computer interaction so painfully slow that potential benefits are lost.

To illustrate these situations, consider the activity of writing a well-structured paragraph with a main idea and appropriate supporting details. It is not possible to specify rules so that a computer could judge whether a student's original paragraph is appropriate. There are examples of lessons that lead a student through this process of paragraph development by asking structured questions that ostensibly produce a main idea and supporting details. The program stores these responses and reassembles them into a finished paragraph. On the surface this seems ideal. However, there is no way the computer can be programmed to guard against the student's responding with nonsense.

In our example, it would be possible to suggest a main idea—for example, "Sometimes telephones in the home are a real nuisance"— and then to ask the student to type several examples to support that sentence. The program must include a long list of keywords and phrases for each anticipated detail that might be suggested in support of the main idea. To identify the idea of "interrupting a bath," keywords such as *bath, shower, bathing, bathroom, john, washing, shampooing, bathtub, shaving, loo,* and others would have to be specified. This requires that all variations and keywords for all plausible instances of telephone nuisance be specified. In programs such as these, the student response is parsed and then compared to the keyword entries. While this is often successful in judging more conventional responses, it sometimes results in accepting a response directly opposed to that desired: "It is *not* a nuisance if it rings while I am taking a shower." In addition, the parsing-comparing procedures are often very slow.

Finally, to restrict the exercise to identifying appropriate supporting details from a predefined list can certainly be done effectively on a computer. However, it dramatically changes the role of the student, the goal of the instruction, and the level of learning from that of our original example.

What's Not Likely . . . Until . . .

What we would like is "intelligent" computer-based instruction that can adapt to the experiences and learning styles of individual students and respond appropriately to student misunderstandings of the subject matter. This requires three things: a model of a "subject matter expert," a model of what the student knows, and a tutor model that is able to compare the student's knowledge with the expert's knowledge and respond appropriately. The computerized "subject matter expert" must be a model of a human problem solver and be able to produce the same outcome as the human problem solver would under the same circumstances. It is not necessary that this "expert" use the same procedures that the human problem solver would, but the results must be like those the human would produce. In the area of English, many learning situations cannot be modelled because there are no well-defined rules or agreement on characteristics that could be used to develop a computer "expert."

Two different types of computer "experts" have been conceived: the "glass-box" expert and the "black-box" expert (Burton and Brown, 1982; Goldstein and Papert, 1977). While both produce responses like those of a human problem solver, they differ on the procedures used to reach the same outcome and on their articulation of the processes they use. The "glass-box" expert is articulate and uses the same procedures that the human would use. The explanation given by the "glass-box" expert and the human would be the same.

The "black-box" expert, on the other hand, uses very different procedures. Since they are different, it would not serve any purpose to articulate them for a user and, as a result, they are kept hidden from view (hence the term "black box"). A good chess playing program is an example of a black box expert. In this type of program, the "expert" looks ahead several exchanges at all possible moves. It then evaluates all those situations to select the move that looks most likely to be successful. Hundreds, possibly even thousands, of moves are generated. This is very different from human chess experts, who tend to select moves based on patterns recognized from experience.

Commercially Available Resources

Many teachers may not realize that there are firms that monitor teachers' software likes and dislikes in much the same way the Nielsen company monitors television show popularity. A survey by one of these companies revealed that one selected group of 400 teachers was using a wide variety of software and held definite opinions on which software they liked best. While preferences varied according to grade level and subject specialty, certain names surfaced fairly consistently. In the language arts, the most often cited at the elementary level were the following:

> Borg Warner's Critical Reading
> Milliken's Language Arts
> MECC's total program
> Radio Shack's IQ Building

At the secondary level, the program list included the following:

> Radio Shack's Scripsit
> Applewriter
> Microsoft's Typing Tutor
> Apple PILOT
> MECC's total program
> Radio Shack's IQ Builder

The elementary favorites are all subject matter related, indicating that they are probably used either to deliver or to supplement regular classroom instruction. The secondary list, on the other hand, consists almost exclusively of products that use the microcomputer as a tool, either for word processing, typing instruction, or programming instruction.

One way of getting information about a software product is through published reviews. In addition to the reviews published in the classroom-oriented computer magazines (*Classroom Computer News, The Computing Teacher, Educational Computer, Educational Technology, Electronic Education, Electronic Learning*), the general computer magazine is also increasing its educational coverage. These magazines include *Compute, Creative Computing, Infoworld,* and *Microcomputing.* While quality of reviews will vary, frequently a new product will be reviewed in several places allowing for comparison.

There are also publications dedicated to software review, including *Courseware Report Card, Journal of Courseware Review, School*

Microware Reviews, Software Reviews, and *Talmis Courseware Ratings.* Local computer user groups (people using the same brand of computer who have put their heads together and experimented) and educational service agencies also offer courseware reviews.

The 1983 Classroom Computer News Directory of Eductional Computing Resources, the first directory of educational computing, offers descriptions of periodicals, professional associations, ongoing projects, and funding. The directory includes a complete yellow pages listing of computer services and products and a one year calendar covering all national and regional events and conferences.

The following commercial houses have produced computer lessons in the language arts at the time of this writing:

> Borg-Warner Education Systems; 600 West University Drive; Arlington Heights, IL 60004-1889
>
> Educulture; 1 Dubuque Plaza, Suite 150; Dubuque, Iowa 52001
>
> Edu-Ware; P.O. Box 22222; Agoura, CA 91301
>
> Hartley Courseware, Inc.; Box 431; Dimondale, MI 48821
>
> MECC (Minnesota Educational Computing Consortium); 2520 Broadway Drive; St. Paul, MN 55113
>
> Milliken Publishing; 1100 Research Blvd.; St. Louis, MO 63132
>
> Random House School Division; 400 Hahn Road; Westminster, MD 21157
>
> Scholastic Inc.; 904 Sylvan Avenue; Englewood Cliffs, NJ 07632
>
> Scott, Foresman and Company; 1900 East Lake Avenue; Glenview, IL 60025
>
> Science Research Associates, Inc.; 155 North Wacker Drive; Chicago, IL 60606

Do-It-Yourself Guidelines to Instructional Development

Someday you may have a need for an instructional lesson that is possible but not available commercially. While the development of an instructional sequence requires a basic knowledge of how students learn, it also requires an educated awareness of the capabilities and limitations of both interactive instruction and the particular machine for which the instruction is designed. This awareness is essential not only in designing computer lessons, but also in evaluating those lessons designed by others.

The basis of an instructional sequence is stated in broad, general terms as a need or requirement—perhaps as a title or a lesson objective. In translating this general need to specifics in developing a computer lesson, we suggest the following initial strategy:

1. Specify objectives: Base the lesson, whether it be expository, discovery, testing, or drill and practice, on clear and detailed objectives. Keep the entire teaching episode in mind even though the computer lesson may be only part of a teaching episode. Make all instructional decisions within the lesson the result of what students do and "say" within the lesson.

2. Analyze the objectives: Determine the specific skills and knowledge needed by the student to attain the objectives. Identify the necessary prerequisite skills.

3. Outline the lesson flow.

4. Script each teaching episode.
   a. Presentation: Write all information and instructions for each teaching episode. Design screen displays to be attractive, easy to read, and relevant.
   b. Questions: Write questions to test whether the objective addressed in the presentation has been attained. Specify notes on question presentation, order, and selection.
   c. Student responses: Specify correct answer(s) and all anticipated incorrect answers.
   d. Computer replies: Write appropriate feedback messages for correct answer(s), anticipated incorrect responses, and unanticipated (but not necessarily incorrect) responses.
   e. Remediation: Write alternative presentation(s) for students who did not attain objective. Write follow-up questions to test comprehension of the material.
   f. Termination: Specify conditions to end the episode.

5. Program the lesson.

6. Refine and debug the lesson: The lesson should be tested with several students who represent those in the intended audience. Test the technical aspects of the lesson as well as the instructional aspects.

7. Document the lesson. Write clear, concise descriptions of the purpose for the lesson, how it operates, and how it could be incorporated into a particular curriculum.

Generic Guidelines for Computer Lessons

In developing and programming the lesson, keep in mind the following generic guidelines.

The lesson should be *relevant*. The instructional goals, teaching strategy, language, and evaluation techniques must be appropriate to the content and the designated student audience.

Design methods to evaluate the effectiveness of the lesson. Systematic evaluation of the lesson should indicate revisions necessary to reach or maintain effectiveness.

The lesson should account for students who use it even though they lack the necessary prerequisite skills. Plan the assessment of prerequisite skills and the instruction, branching, and feedback given to these students.

Develop the fundamental lesson sequence for the student who is able to grasp *and* demonstrate the indicated knowledge or skills. For students who need or request it, make available additional information, explanation, and application.

Although the length of a teaching cycle is the responsibility of the designer, research has indicated that shorter cycles (avoiding arbitrary conciseness) are more effective than longer cycles.

The lesson should be *easy to use*. Keep in mind the intended audience and the environment. The lesson should be easy to use for the novice without being tedious for the experienced user. Explain and account for the computer environment as well as for the content. Keep the technical skill level required of the user to a minimum without compromising the content or the creative and effective use of the medium.

Determine an appropriate length of the lesson. If the lesson is designed to be completed in more than one session, it should include provisions to begin where the last session ended, perhaps with a succinct review (or at least an indication) of material studied earlier. Do not require the student to begin again. One strategy might be to ask questions about earlier material followed by an option (and/or a recommendation) to review before starting the new material.

The lesson should be *bullet-proofed*. Design lessons to avoid terminating accidentally, inhibiting student progress, accepting inappropriate responses without appropriate messages, and displaying computer "default" messages that are incomprehensible to nontechnical users.

Test programs thoroughly before using them in an instructional setting. This suggests several strategies:

1. Use the lesson as you think it was intended. If the program does not work appropriately in the best of circumstances, it is not properly "bullet-proofed."
2. Try "unexpected" responses wherever possible. This includes testing the range of possible content-related answers as well as testing the computer environment. For example, what happens when you respond with numbers, punctuation, or blanks when asked your name?
3. Always test the program with students who are from the intended audience. Never rely solely on your own testing.

The lesson should be *interactive*. Test each skill and knowledge implied by the objective after the presentation as well as later in the program, either as prerequisite to a new concept or as part of a posttest. Avoid passive responding. Increase the incentive for correct responses. Retest students on missed concepts. Wherever possible, use new questions rather than simply repeating the original ones. Retest concepts after corrective measures have been taken as well as after a delay to be sure the student has not simply memorized the answer.

Design a strategy that will permit the student to continue even if he or she was unable to answer the way you expected. A well-designed program will not permit a student to get "caught" in a section and not be able to progress. Allow the student maximum control over the flow that is consistent with your objectives.

The lesson should be *diagnostic*. Lessons should differentiate between students and provide individualized feedback, remediation, and branching based on how they responded. Lessons that do not differentiate gain nothing over conventional large group instruction.

The lesson should be *attractive*. Plan text and graphics for emphasis and readability. Vary screen displays to increase attention.

Many computers offer color, sound, and animation. Include them if they are pedagogically sound, not simply because they are "cute." Otherwise, they will soon lose their novelty effect and frustrate the user.

Developing computer applications to English and language arts instruction has become an exciting, even profitable, activity for some classroom teachers. The same thorough grounding in general how-to's of instructional design such as the foregoing should also be referred to in a thoughtful evaluation of already-produced computer lessons. Before teachers can make reasonable judgments as to the efficacy of a lesson or series of lessons for their students, they need to be aware of what "good" computer software looks like.

Chapter 3 Scenario

The scenario to end this chapter again involves Duane Ridley, whom we left in chapter 1 after his class had been visited by Professor Richards, the "educational computer expert" from the college where Duane teaches part-time in order to supplement his salary from the high school. As a result of the positive feedback that Duane received from students and fellow teachers after that visit, Duane has been working fairly regularly with Professor Richards. Duane knows enough about the nature of programming to be certain that the role of programmer is not for him. Nevertheless, he feels an interest in the potential of computer-assisted instruction. His conversations with Professor Richards have reinforced for Duane the belief that faculty in all academic areas must develop a basic "computer literacy" so that they can communicate, as subject specialists, with the programmers who develop the software for academic use. This is true whether the software developers are professionals or simply students who are seeking new programming challenges.

As we encounter Duane this time, he is in Professor Richards' office. It is late afternoon, and Duane has just arrived on campus after finishing his eighth-hour class at the high school. The two of them have been joined by two seniors from the college—data processing majors who need programming projects to complete as part of a course assignment. Professor Richards has been recounting to them the tale of the program written by one of last semester's graduate students—the program that needed repair after being field tested with Duane's ninth-graders. Duane's students were able to omit needed capitalization without penalty but were subjected to capricious "error" statements simply because the program's method of response input had been poorly designed.

"The problems generated by Duane's students really proved depressing to that programmer for a few days," Professor Richards informed his listeners. "But pretty soon he realized that such field testing was the best way in which to de-bug his programs. In the end, the adaptations he made resulted in a very useful program, which has subsequently been field-tested at other schools with great success."

"I'm glad you recalled that war story," Duane said to the professor. "It may be just the thing these fellows need to hear, because I've laid a doozie on them just recently."

"They'd just begun to tell me about it," Professor Richards interrupted. "That's what brought last semester's experience to mind. Now . . . just what is it that you want?"

Duane settled into a chair and began to describe the type of software he had hoped could be developed.

"As you know, I work with both ninth and twelfth grade students at the high school. I have found many drills and instructional games involving grammar or composition skills that work well with the ninth graders, but those seniors require instruction of a more complex nature. Also, many of my seniors are college-bound, and I like to challenge them with assignments that involve cognitive skills at the higher levels. To date, I really haven't found any computer-assisted instruction that is working at that level. I was hoping that these fellows would be able to develop a tutorial program that I could use with those students."

Professor Richards nodded, looked at the two data processing students, and then looked back at Duane. "You know, of course, that while your question sounds very simple, it involves programming skills of a very high level."

"I know," Duane responded. "But I thought that—by working together—we could combine my subject matter expertise with their programming experience and come up with something really worthwhile . . . maybe even the basis for a professional publication." He winked at the students, knowing how those last two words always managed to catch the attention of academics in a "publish or perish" setting.

Professor Richards shifted in his chair. "Please continue."

Duane picked up the conversation. "These seniors who'll go on to college will all be required to take Freshman Composition. And, as a part-time instructor of that subject myself, I see the greatest potential for a project lying in the development of a tutorial program that would allow students to improve their skills at writing unified, coherent paragraphs, paragraphs in which a single main idea clearly ties the unit together, in which all sentences work to develop that idea, and in which no sentences distract from that idea."

Professor Richards groaned. "You don't ask much, do you? You want to allow initial input to be so variable that any idea named by the student can be a main idea?"

"Not any idea," Duane interjected. "It has to be narrow enough in scope to be a workable main idea."

"Will they have had previous instruction on how to limit ideas to this workable scope?"

"Yes," Duane replied. "But, of course, the opportunity to review that instruction should also be built into this program."

"You must help us out here, subject matter expert. What is it that defines an idea as sufficiently narrow in scope to be the main idea of *a paragraph? Are there particular traits that can be identified, so that the program can test for their presence or absence?"*

"It's funny you should ask. This seems to be one of those concepts whose presence or absence is easily recognizable. I can always tell if a paragraph has one or lacks one. But when I'm asked to tell you some concrete traits which could (1) be identified and (2) be the objects of a computer search, I find myself hard pressed to do so."

"Remember that, Duane. It may be the best answer available for those English teachers who fear that, someday, they may be replaced by computers. It also underscores the importance for teachers in all subject areas to take the time to apply to their teaching the educational principles about concept identification, levels of complexity, examples and nonexamples, and the like."

"Okay, you're right. That won't work the way I want it to. But that still doesn't help these two fellows who need a programming project."

"Well, Duane, let's try to consider some other aspects of composition that do have such well-defined traits that can be modelled on a computer. What about the expansion of that main idea? Would your students need instruction on plot development, for example?"

"Could be. Keep talking."

"Well, these fellows need to get some pretty high-level programming experience. Can you think of a program that would branch in any of several directions to offer instruction or to ask questions based on input supplied by the student?"

"Sure. That has definite possibilities. The program could present the student with some characters, a setting, and a few suggestions about relationships among them. Then the student would be free to build a plot."

"But a student could do that with pen and paper, Duane. What could be done uniquely with the computer in this situation?"

"Aha! The student could be forced to do this sequentially. You're right about the pen and paper. I use this type of assignment regularly with my students, and then allow them thirty to forty minutes to build a story. Some do a great job, but others get so wrapped up in describing the characters that no plot ever develops. A few start to develop a plot, but get so wrapped up in trying to be clever that the essence of the plot changes three or four times, never coming to a resolution."

"Okay, Duane. I think we're on to something. The student suggests the beginning of a plot, then is asked certain questions in order to be sure that the plot development continues and doesn't fall by the wayside."

"But that still involves an awful lot of options. Ten students may suggest ten different plots. Can the program respond to input which is so open-ended?"

"Well, Duane, that depends. You can limit the number of possible student inputs by suggesting three or four plot directions, then identifying a bank of key words that would appear for each of those possibilities. Then the input would be parsed for those key words, and subsequent branching would be based upon the presence or absence of those words."

"Sounds like lots of work for the programmer. What other option is available?"

"Well, you can brainstorm every possible plot you think might be developed, again identify some key terms that would be associated with each, then search and branch accordingly."

"I guess that first plan doesn't sound so terrible after all. Are you up for it, fellows?" Duane asked as he turned to the programmers present.

Their upraised thumbs said it all.

4 Evaluating Computer Courseware

Now that you have the courseware, what's next? You know how computer courseware could be incorporated into your particular style of teaching. You know where and how to acquire courseware applicable to your lesson content. How do you tell the good programs from the not-so-good programs? How do you distinguish the courseware that is acceptable "as-is" from the courseware that would be acceptable only if modified? Isn't courseware evaluation similar to evaluating textbooks or other print material? Isn't what you see what you get?

If you have ever served on a textbook evaluation committee or spent time browsing through exhibitors' book displays, you have probably developed the ability to decide whether or not a book fits your teaching needs after a fairly quick and cursory examination. A single page-through will reveal to experienced teachers whether the reader, literature anthology, or grammar handbook in question is suitable for their students.

Not so the case with computer courseware. Because of the nature of the instructional medium (the exchange of "dialogue" between student and computer lesson), a single "page-through" will not reveal all aspects of content presentation, interaction required of the student, instructional quality, or ease of operation. As a matter of fact, several runs through a computer lesson are required to fully absorb both the content and the effect that the lesson has on the user. As long a period as fourteen hours has been spent studying a single lesson by a teacher who wanted to become as familiar with the lesson design as the original programmer.

Such intense scrutiny is neither possible nor desirable with most classroom courseware. However, a thorough familiarity with a proposed lesson is not only desirable, it is essential if the quality of your instruction is to be maintained. As the teacher responsible for the instruction delivered in your classroom, you need to know if the lesson is polite in tone of feedback; if the material is fun and challenging, not boring or "cutesy;" if the content is appropriate for your students; if the directions are clear and easily accessible; if the content can be integrated with previous classroom instruction; if the content is free of race, sex, or other stereotypes; or if the level of each question is consistent with the level of presentation.

Resources for the Evaluator

The need for developing a systematized or structured procedure for evaluating instructional computer courseware is a very real one. The new industry producing programs to aid or substitute for content-area instruction needs appraisal and constructive criticism by experienced evaluators. In particular, application of the computer to English instruction, still in its infant stages, should have its own informed evaluators. If the instructional quality of a computerized English or reading lesson is poor, it is because no one has demanded that it be improved. Likewise, if the teacher's manual for a computerized lesson is confusing or unintelligible, it is because no one has specified how it should be revised. Now, while the courseware development industry is young, open to suggestion, and sensitive to competition, classroom teachers have an opportunity to influence curriculum development—but only if they know what they are talking about.

Because of the proliferation of instructional software packages by a variety of large and small publishers who have been hesitant to release preview materials to potential purchases, the use of indepth software evaluations has become a necessity for computer-using educators. Computer software evaluations/reviews are being published in a variety of sources, most notably in educational computing journals such as *Classroom Computer News, The Computing Teacher, Creative Computing, On Computing, Educational Technology,* and *Electronic Learning.* These periodicals are available by subscription to individuals or institutions.

Evaluations of computer software are also available in the newsbulletins of those consortiums formed to serve computer-using teachers' needs. Two such sources are the Minnesota Educational Computing Consortium (MECC) or the MICRO-Ideas Project in Illinois. These newsbulletins are issued to specific membership mailing lists, limiting the availability of their software reviews. Another source of software evaluation is the Resources in Computer Education (RICE) database, developed by the Computer Technology Program at the Northwest Regional Educational Laboratory (NWERL). The RICE file is accessed through the BRS, Inc., School Practices

Information Network (SPIN) and is available only to those who have a BRS search password, a contract with Bibliographic Retrieval Services (a commercial database vendor in Latham, New York), and a microcomputer and modem to access information files.

The Microcomputer Index, a file available through another large, commercial database vendor called DIALOG, is a subject and abstract guide to microcomputer articles from over twenty-five periodical sources such as *Byte, InfoWorld, Personal Computing, Interface Age, Creative Computing,* and *Softside.* Included are general articles about the microcomputer world, book reviews, software reviews, discussions of applications in various milieu, and descriptions of new computer products. The Index provides information about new modems or printers, as well as reviews of software packages.

Evaluation Guidelines

Several thoughtful evaluation instruments have been designed to assist those teachers interested in making their own informed decisions with regard to the computer courseware they provide their students. One of the earliest is *Evaluating Materials for Teaching with a Computer* by J. Richard Dennis, No. 5e in the Illinois Series on Educational Application of Computers developed at the University of Illinois. Dennis provides both a rationale for evaluating courseware and a sample courseware evaluation worksheet that suggests multiple lesson executions.

Another set of evaluation guidelines is offered by the Instructional Affairs Committee of the National Council of Teachers of Mathematics. Rather than attempting to employ numerical ratings to generate purchase-rejection decisions, the *NCTM Software Evaluation Checklist* can be adapted to reflect a given user's selection of criteria and focuses on the issues critical to those decisions.

Still another evaluation instrument is the *Evaluator's Guide for Microcomputer-Based Packages* developed by MicroSIFT (Microcomputer Software and Information for Teachers), a project of the Computer Technology Program of the Northwest Regional Educational Laboratory in Portland, Oregon. The MicroSIFT clearinghouse for microcomputer-based educational software and courseware developed the *Evaluator's Guide* to provide background information and description/evaluation forms to aid teachers and other educators in evaluating software before purchasing, and to be used as a supplement to preservice and inservice courses concerned with the development or use of computer-based applications.

The National Council of Teachers of English has formed an Instructional Technology Committee to establish, as part of its charge, a set of guidelines to help language arts teachers select main frame and microcomputer programs for use in their classrooms, and to encourage publishers and software producers to develop materials that both meet the instructional aims of language arts educators and use the interactive capabilities of the computer to enhance learning. Criteria in the NCTE guidelines focus on areas that are common to most types of educational courseware and are included in the other evaluation instruments. They differ, however, in that they offer criteria specific to evaluating the appropriateness of courseware for the teaching of language arts.

Which Guidelines to Use?

Because the classroom teacher is the only one who knows the sometimes strange and wonderful mixture of individual learning styles, personality traits, and cognitive stages that students represent, no one set of guidelines can provide all of the criteria to judge the quality of computer courseware for a particular set of students. Nor can any set of criteria completely reflect all the nuances of the purpose of a lesson or individual instructional situation. When shopping for a new car, only the prospective buyer is aware of all the criteria that his or her purchase must meet. All a new car shopping guide or tips from interested friends can attempt to do is to raise points to consider before purchasing. No one but the buyer is totally aware of his or her own particular situation.

A list of thoughtful evaluation criteria can and should benefit teachers who utilize courseware by pointing out a program's strengths as well as its weaknesses. Through the experience gained in preparing detailed courseware evaluations, teachers can increase their awareness of what to look for in high-quality courseware and of their roles in implementing the lessons with their students. As teachers' awareness increases, they will become more knowledgeable and discriminating when selecting courseware, which should in turn, encourage developers to continue to improve the quality of their products.

The evaluative issues that may be inferred from the various guidelines instruments described above represent state-of-the-art knowledge, experience, and intuition regarding what constitutes a "good" computer program. A cursory look at one of the evaluation instruments may give you the feeling that more questions are raised about evaluating instructional computer programs than any reasonable person would ever care to have answered. That is because evaluative criteria in the area of computer courseware are both numerous and tentative. Many are expressions of group or personal values, and would thus be judged to be very important by some users while being viewed as unimportant by others. It is expected that a given user will assign greater weight to some criteria than to others. It is assumed that the proper task of the user is to select and weigh the criteria used in his or her evaluation of a program. The role of any set of guidelines is to guide the decision maker, supporting the thoughtful review of an issue.

Chapter 4 Scenario

The scenario to end this chapter is set at the annual state meeting of English teachers. Here, Karen Young (we met her in chapter 2)—at the request of her advisor from the university—is presenting a session about the various kinds of software available for use in English classes.

As is often the case at these sessions, she is limited to having only one microcomputer available on which the various programs can be demonstrated. Nevertheless, she has prepared a series of handouts for those in attendance. Some of the handouts simply list print and software resources; others show examples from several programs.

In attendance at this session are both Janice Doan* and Duane Ridley (familiar from chapters 1 and 3). They are part of a standing-room-only audience, reflecting the fact that microcomputers are no longer the sole domain of math, science, or business departments. Karen's topic has drawn a large crowd, in spite of the fact that six other presentations are going on simultaneously, two of which involve "teacher burnout" and "surviving on reduced budgets."

In any event, Karen manages to display three separate types of software during the thirty minutes allotted for her presentation. It is during the fifteen minute question and answer period that she encounters queries from Janice and Duane, which set the stage for some lively exchanges about software.

Janice is one of the first to raise her hand when Karen stops speaking. She briefly presents her background, mentioning that she teaches

---

*Janice Doan teaches fourth-grade English in a rural midwest town of approximately 16,500 population. She has a B.A. from a state university, plus eight hours of graduate credit in elementary education, and is in her third year of teaching. The principal of her school has been talking with marketing representatives from three microcomputer companies. Janice fears RIF-ing, but she is willing to learn about computers if that will enhance her potential to remain employed. Also, she has seen demonstrations of computer-assisted instruction while taking a graduate class.

elementary school in a rural town and that her principal seems interested in the purchase of microcomputers for their building.

"My question," Janice continues, "involves those sales representatives who have been visiting our school. How do I know what I can or can't believe? At least, when textbook salespersons come around, I can leaf through the books, look at the supplemental materials available, and have a pretty concrete idea of costs. With these people selling computers, I have no idea about the strengths or weaknesses of the software available. And if we purchase the computers from Company X, will we be limited to purchasing software from the same company? Or will programs produced by Company Y be compatible with that hardware? I really need some guidelines."

Karen nearly glowed as Janice finished her question. Addressing the group as a whole, she said, "Please let me attest to the fact that I have never before seen this woman. She is not my sister and I have not paid her to come here and ask this perfect question." That drew a chuckle from the assembly, after which Karen continued.

"The point Janice made in her question is essential, especially considering the costs involved when a school or a district decides to purchase six or ten or fifty microcomputers. Once they have been bought, that's it. No school board is likely to approve the expense of replacing them with the products of a different manufacturer in two years. This is why it is so important that faculty from all academic areas and all grade levels work with the administration to develop some key questions to be asked of marketing representatives. You are right in wondering about the availability of software and the compatability of the hardware with programs from other sources. It is also important to learn which items are included in the prices quoted, and which are optional. The visual quality of the screen, the size of the memory, the potential for expanding the memory, the speed with which input is processed and output is printed . . . all of these are key questions. And you may find it hard to believe, but it just happens that Professor Swank, my advisor from Midwest University, has written a monograph listing these concerns. A copy of the monograph is here on the display table and you are all welcome to examine it when this session ends. Individual copies are available for seventy-five cents from the College of Education at the University. I'll write the address here on the board."

Following an appreciative murmur that rippled through the crowd, Duane Ridley gained Karen's attention and rose to comment.

"I appreciate the answer you gave to the young lady concerned about evaluating commercially prepared software as well as hardware. *I know I've shared her frustrations many times, even though I teach at the secondary and college levels. I would simply like to share one additional thought with those of you in this room. No matter what type of hardware your school or district may purchase, don't feel confined to the use of commerically-prepared software. I have recently had occasion to work with personnel from our own local college, both faculty and students, to develop software for use with my own students. I was amazed not only at the programming expertise in my own community, but also at the other benefits which arose when I started working cooperatively with the people from the college. As college people visited our building on one occasion after another, informal dialogues began to develop among our teachers, our students, the college teachers, and the college students—even between our students and our teachers!*

"I encourage each of you to look around you when you return to your schools. You never know what talents lie untapped in those students and colleagues you pass daily in the halls."

Cries of "hear, hear!" came from several spots in the room. Karen picked up on that, looked at the clock and at the nervous presenter waiting in the hall for his chance to set up for the next session, and raised her voice. "I can think of no better note on which to end. Thank you all for coming!"

References

Introduction

Barth, Rod. "ERIC/RCS Report: An Annotated Bibliography of Readings for the Computer Novice and the English Teacher." *English Journal* 68, no. 1 (January 1979): 68. (ERIC No. EJ 195 994)

Gleason, Gerald T. "Micro Computers in Education: The 'State of the Art.'" *Educational Technology* 21, no. 3(1981): 7–18. (ERIC No. EJ 244 284)

Jaycox, Kathy. *Computer Applications in the Teaching of English.* The Illinois Series on Educational Application of Computers, no. 19e. Urbana, Ill.: University of Illinois College of Education, 1980. (ERIC Document Reproduction Service No. ED 183 196)

Lacy, Dan. "Print, Television, Computers, and English." *ADE Bulletin* 72 (Summer 1982): 34–38. (ERIC No. EJ 265 659)

Nold, Ellen. "Fear and Trembling." *College Composition and Communication* 26(October 1975): 269–73. (ERIC No. EJ 135 934)

O'Donnell, Holly. "Computer Literacy, Part I: Classroom Applications." *The Reading Teacher* 35, no. 4(January 1982): 490–4. (ERIC No. EJ 256 302)

O'Donnell, Holly. "Computer Literacy, Part II: Classroom Applications." *The Reading Teacher* 35, no. 5(February 1982): 614–7. (ERIC No. EJ 257 752)

Schwartz, Helen J. "Monsters and Mentors: Computer Applications for Humanistic Education." *College English* 44, no. 2 (February 1982): 141–52. (ERIC No. EJ 257 857)

Wresch, William. "Computers in English Class: Finally beyond Grammar and Spelling." *College English* 44, no. 5(September 1982): 483–90. (ERIC No. EJ 266 969)

Chapter One

Auten, Anne. "So You Want to Buy a Microcomputer: A Guide to Purchasing." *English Journal* 71, no. 6(October 1982): 56–7. (ERIC No. EJ 268 158)

Auten, Anne, J. Richard Dennis, and Sally Standiford. *Making Sense of Computer Applications in the English Classroom.* Resource Packet. Urbana, Ill.: ERIC Clearinghouse on Reading and Communication Skills, 1982. ($5.00)

Braun, Ludwig. "Help! What Computer Should I Buy???" *Run: Computer Education.* Monterey, Calif.: Brooks/Cole Publishing Co., 1983.

Burns, Hugh. *A Writer's Tool: Computing as a Mode of Inventing.* Monterey, Calif.: Brooks/Cole Publishing Co., 1983. (ERIC Document Reproduction Service No. ED 193 693)

Frederick, Franz J. *Guide to Microcomputers.* Washington, D.C.: Association for Educational Communications and Technology, 1980. (ERIC Document Reproduction Service No. ED 192 818)

Samojeden, Elizabeth. "The Use of Computers in the Classroom." Paper presented at the Minnesota Reading Association Conference, Ossew, Minnesota, November 1982. (ERIC Accession No. CS 006 960)

Staples, Betsy. "Van Helps Schools Select the Right Computer." *Run: Computer Education.* Monterey, Calif.: Brooks/Cole Publishing Co., 1983.

Chapter Two

Bork, Alfred, and Stephen D. Franklin. "The Role of Personal Computer Systems in Education." *AEDS Journal* 13, no. 1 (Fall 1979): 17–30. (ERIC No. EJ 223 569)

Burns, Hugh. *Stimulating Rhetorical Invention in English Composition through Computer-Assisted Instruction.* Austin: University of Texas, 1979. (ERIC Document Reproduction Service No. ED 188 245)

Cherry, L. L., and W. Vesterman. *Writing Tools–The STYLE and DICTION Programs.* Murray Hill, N. J.: Bell Laboratories, 1980.

Gerrard, Lisa. *Using a Computerized Text-Editor in Freshman Composition.* Los Angeles, Calif.: UCLA Writing Programs, 1982. (ERIC No. CS 207 416)

Halpern, Jeanne W. "Effects of Dictation/Word Processing Systems on Teaching Writing." Paper presented at the annual meeting of the Conference on College Composition and Communication, San Francisco, California, March 1982. (ERIC Document Reproduction Service No. ED 215 357)

MacDonald, Nina H., and others. "The Writer's Workbench: Computer Aids for Text Analysis." *IEEE/Transactions on Communications* COM-30, no. 1 (January 1982): 105–10.

Nicholl, James R. *How Microcomputers May Redefine English Teaching.* Cullowhee, N. C.: Department of English, Western Carolina University, 1982.

Rauch, Margaret, and Elizabeth Samojeden. Computer-Assited Instruction: One Aid for Teachers of Reading. 1981. (ERIC Document Reproduction Service No. ED 204 702)

Schwartz, Mimi. "Computers and the Teaching of Writing." *Educational Technology* 22, no. 11(November 1982): 27–9.

Chapter Three

Arms, Valerie. "The Computer Kids and Composition." Paper presented at the annual meeting of the Conference on College Composition and Communication, San Francisco, California, March 1982. (ERIC Document Reproduction Service No. ED 217 489)

Auten, Anne. "Computer Literacy, Part III: CRT Graphics." *The Reading Teacher* 35, no. 8 (May 1982): 966–69. (ERIC No. EJ 261 425)

Bradley, Virginia N. "Improving Students' Writing with Microcomputers." *Language Arts* 59, no. 7 (October 1982): 732–43. (ERIC No. EJ 269 739)

Brebner, Ann, and others. Teaching Elementary Reading by CMI and CAI. 1980. (ERIC Document Reproduction Service No. ED 198 793)

Burton, Richard R., and John Seely Brown. "An Investigation of Computer Coaching for Informal Learning Activities." In *Intelligent Tutoring Systems.* Edited by D. Sleeman and J. S. Brown. New York: Academic Press, 1982.

Cottey, Patricia. An Overview of the Computer as Teacher: A Progress Report of a Research Project to Introduce Diagnostic Testing and Computerized Instruction into the Composition Program at Northeast Missouri State University. (ERIC Document Reproduction Service No. ED 217 485)

Cronnell, Bruce. *Computer-Based Practice in Editing.* Los Alamitos, Calif.: Southwest Regional Laboratory, 1982. (ERIC Reproduction Service No. ED 220 869)

Cronnell, Bruce, and Ann Humes. "Using Microcomputers for Composition Instruction." Paper presented at the annual meeting of the Conference on College Composition and Communication, Dallas, Texas, March 1981. (ERIC Document Reproduction Service No. ED 203 872)

Garson, James W. "The Case against Multiple Choice." *The Computing Teacher* (December 1979).

Goldstein, I., and S. Papert. "Artificial Intelligence, Language, and the Study of Knowledge." *Cognitive Science* 1, no. 1 (1977): 1–21.

Hennings, Dorothy Grant. "Input: Enter the Word-Processing Computer." *Language Arts* 58, no. 1 (January 1981): 18–22. (ERIC No. EJ 240 325)

Humes, Ann. *Computer Instruction on Generating Ideas for Writing Description.* Los Alamitos, Calif.: Southwest Regional Laboratory, 1982. (ERIC Document Reproduction Service No. ED 220 868)

Jaycox, Kathy. "Ware, Oh, Ware Might an English Class Go?" *Illinois English Bulletin* (Winter 1979): 21–27.

Kingman, James C. "Designing Good Educational Software." *Creative Computing* 7, no. 10 (October 1981): 72ff. (ERIC No. EJ 252 711)

Marcus, Stephen. "Compupoem: CAI for Writing and Studying Poetry." *The Computing Teacher* 8, no. 3 (March 1982): 28–31.

Mason, George E., and Jay S. Blanchard. *Computer Applications in Reading.* Reston, Va.: International Reading Association, 1979. (ERIC Document Reproduction Service No. ED 173 771)

Schwartz, Helen J. "A Computer Program for Invention and Feedback." Paper presented at the annual meeting of the Conference on College Composition and Communication, San Francisco, California, March 1982. (ERIC Document Reproduction Service No. 214 177)

Southwell, Michael G. "Using Computer-Assisted Instruction for Developmental Writing." *AEDS Journal* 16, no. 2 (Winter 1982): 80–91.

Thompson, Barbara. "Computers in Reading: A Review of Applications and Implications." *Educational Technology* 20, no. 8 (August 1980): 38–41. (ERIC No. EJ 232 552)

Wall, Shavaun M., and Nancy E. Taylor. "Using Interactive Computer Programs in Teaching Higher Conceptual Skills: An Approach to Instruction in Writing." *Educational Technology* (February 1982): 13–17. (ERIC No. EJ 261 908)

Wresch, William. *Prewriting, Writing, and Editing by Computer.* Marinette: University of Wisconsin, 1982. (ERIC Document Reproduction Service No. ED 213 045)

Chapter Four

Auten, Anne, J. Richard Dennis, and Sally Standiford. *Making Sense of Computer Applications in the English Classroom.* Resource Packet. Urbana, Ill.: ERIC Clearinghouse on Reading and Communication Skills, 1982. ($5.00)

Bell, Arthur H. "The Trouble with Software: An English Teacher's Lament." *Curriculum Review* 21, no. 5 (December 1982): 497–9.

Burns, Hugh. "Pandora's Chip." *Pipeline* (Fall 1981): 15–16, 49.

Delf, Robert M. "Primer for Purchasing Software." *American School and University* (July 1981): 44–45. (ERIC No. EJ 249 872)

Dennis J. Richard. *Evaluating Materials for Teaching with a Computer.* The Illinois Series on Educational Applications of Computers, no. 5e. Urbana, Ill.: University of Illinois College of Education, 1979. (ERIC Document Reproduction Service No. ED 200 228)

Douglas, Shirley, and Gary Neights. Instructional Software Selection: A Guide to Instructional Microcomputer Software. (ERIC Document Reproduction Service No. ED 205 201)

Evaluator's Guide for Microcomputer Based Instructional Packages. Eugene: University of Oregon Department of Computer Information Science, International Council for Computers in Education, 1982. (ERIC Document Reproduction Service No. ED 206 330)

Heck, William P., Jerry Johnson, and Robert J. Kansky. *Guidelines for Evaluating Computerized Instructional Materials.* Reston, VA: National Council of Teachers of Mathematics, 1981.

Komoski, P. Kenneth. "The Educational Revolution Is Not in the Chips." *Education Week,* 21 April 1982, p. 24, 20.

Microcomputer Courseware/Microprocessor Games. EPIE Materials Report 98/99m. New York: Educational Products Information Exchange Institute, 1982.

Software Review. Westport, Conn.: Microform Review Inc., 1982.

Glossary

authoring system   A set of programs to help authors organize and implement instructional lessons. Such a system might include programs to help the author design questions, feedback, and remediation by prompting the author with specific cues. Usually, the author does not need to know the specific programming commands to implement the instructions.

BASIC   *Beginners All-purpose Symbolic Instruction Code.* A common programming language available on most microcomputers.

bit   The smallest amount of information which can be processed. A *BInary digiT*, either a zero (0) or a one (1). A different sequence of bits can be used to code different letters or numerals which can be processed by the computer. For example, the sequence 0110101 might be the letter A. Most computers are designed to manipulate information that is coded in binary form.

bug   An error in the hardware (e.g., equipment malfunction) or the software (program error).

byte   Eight bits (usually). Often used to represent an alpha-numeric character or a number between 0 and 255.

CAI   *Computer Assisted (or Aided) Instruction.* Generally, the process of using the computer to deliver instruction through preprogrammed lessons (called "canned" programs). Other CAI related initials include:

CAL	Computer Assisted Learning
CBI	Computer Based Instruction
CBE	Computer Based Education
CMI	Computer Managed Instruction
EAC	Educational Applications of Computers
IAC	Instructional Applications of Computers

canned program   A complete, ready-to-use program which is usually stored on a cassette tape or floppy diskette.

courseware   A combination of "course" and "software" that identifies programs with an educational content or use.

CRT   *Cathode Ray Tube*, a television type screen for displaying data, graphics, etc.

data base   A collection of data stored in an organized manner. It can be made up of numeric and/or text data.

disk (disc)   A circular piece of material on which information can be stored magnetically.

diskette   A small (usually 5.25 or 8 inch diameter) disk made of flexible (floppy) material. One small floppy disk can hold all the information found in a large dictionary.

disk drive (system)   A peripheral device which is used to store information on or retrieve information from a disk.

hard copy   Computer output on paper.

hardware   The physical components of a computer including the central processor, memory devices, and peripheral equipment.

input   Information or data entered into the computer through such devices as keyboard, punched cards, magnetic tape, disk, graphics tablets, light pens, joy sticks, etc.

I/O   Input/Output.

K   A mathematical prefix signifying one thousand (1000). In computer terminology, K is used with a number to specify the memory size of a computer. For example, 64K equals 64,000 which means that the computer memory is approximately 64,000 bytes (or characters) of data.

keyboard   A computer input device that resembles a typewriter.

memory   The portion of a computer which stores data. Many computers have a small, fast primary memory and a larger but slower secondary memory.

microcomputer   A small self-contained computer containing a microprocessor which can execute instructions. The microprocessor chip is the brain of the computer containing memory, logic, and control elements.

modem   A *MO*dulator-*DEM*odulator device that allows a computer to communicate over telephone lines.

monitor   A video output unit that uses a Cathode Ray Tube for display.

output   Information leaving the terminal. Some output devices include printers, disk drives, music or voice synthesizers, CRT screens, etc.

peripheral   Any device which can send information to or receive information from a computer.

program   A detailed set of instructions which describes a process. The program is written in a computer language chosen for the particular process being described. For example, COBOL (*CO*mmon *B*usiness *O*riented *L*anguage) is often used for business applications; FORTRAN (*FOR*mula *TRAN*slator) is used for scientific applications.

RAM   *R*andom *A*ccess *M*emory is the main memory of the computer. Data may be stored in or retrieved from or changed in RAM. Information stored in RAM is lost when the machine is turned off.

ROM   *R*ead *O*nly *M*emory is that in which the information is permanently stored (usually by the manufacturer). This information cannot be changed.

scroll   Text displayed can be moved up or down for viewing.

software   All programs which the computer uses.

teletex   Systems similar to videotext but only for receiving information. The user cannot send information.

text editor   Computer or word processing program that allows text manipulation such as additions, deletions, or alterations.

timesharing   A method of using a computer in which many people use the computer at the same time.

videotex   A general term for systems which combine the computer, CRT, and telephone in various ways to transmit text and simple graphics to a simple receiver. Such systems are interactive and usually designed so that untrained users can transmit information easily. Current systems are being used for news, sports, advertising, library services, etc.

word processing   The use of computers to format papers, documents, reports and other text materials. The text is typed and stored in computer memory where it can be changed, deleted, added to, or retrieved.

Authors

Anne Auten is coordinator of User Services for the ERIC Clearinghouse on Reading and Communication Skills and has taught junior high school English. Recent publications include articles on reading/writing relationships and computer literacy in *The Reading Teacher, Journal of Reading,* and *English Journal.* She has been a convention presenter for the National Council of Teachers of English, the Illinois Association of Teachers of English, and the International Reading Association and is active in preservice teacher education in information resources.

Kathleen Jaycox is dean of Continuing Education and Community Services at Morton College, Cicero. A former high school English teacher, she has taught English at Western Illinois University and Lincoln College, Illinois, and is a member of the National Council of Teachers of English and the Conference on College Composition and Communication. She has been elected to Outstanding Young Women of America and Who's Who in the Midwest and was a participant in the American Association of Community and Junior Colleges "Leaders of the 80s" Project.

Sally N. Standiford is a visiting assistant professor in Instructional Applications of Computers, Department of Secondary Education, University of Illinois at Urbana-Champaign. She has been an administrator of the City Colleges of Chicago PLATO Project, an instructional design specialist for Control Data Corporation, and has authored reports from both the Center for the Study of Reading and the Computer-based Education Research Laboratory at the University of Illinois. With a major interest in preservice and inservice teacher education, she has been active in the National Council of Teachers of English and the Illinois Association of Teachers of English.